Some Birds and Mammals of the Woodlar

by Kenneth Lilly

© THE MEDICI SOCIETY LTD · LONDON · 1997   Printed in England   ISBN 0 85503 045 3

Red Fox (*Vulpes vulpes*) DOG FAMILY

Size: Head and body about 24 in. (61 cm). Tail about 16 in. (40 cm). Height to the shoulder 12–14 in. (30–36 cm). The female, or 'vixen', is usually slightly smaller and without the cheek ruffs of the male, or 'dog fox'. Weight approximately 12–15 lb (5.4–6.8 kg).

Breeding: The vixen produces her one litter a year in about April. There are usually four to six cubs. They are born in an 'earth' which is really no more than a deep hole the foxes dig for themselves, or, if one is available, they take over a disused badger set or enlarge a rabbit burrow.

The cubs are born blind and although their eyes open when they are about ten days old, they will remain in the earth for the first four weeks of their lives. At this age, they will emerge from the earth and can be seen playing near the entrance during the evening. During this 'playtime' they will quickly learn to obey the commands of the vixen, to come to her immediately she calls, to 'freeze' like a statue when hunting, or to run for cover if danger threatens. When these lessons have been learnt, they will then accompany the vixen on her nightly hunting expeditions to learn the highly skilled art of hunting.

The cubs will leave their parents when they are about two months old, by which time they should have learnt enough of the hunting skills to be able to fend for themselves.

Habits: The fox is justly known as a very resourceful hunter. If unable to approach near enough to its prey to attempt a kill, it will leap about, chasing its tail in seemingly playful mood. Its prey, often a rabbit, will be so intrigued by this unusual behaviour that it will be quite unaware that the playful fox is getting slowly nearer and nearer until, suddenly, too late . . . with a lightning dash, the fox is rewarded with its next meal.

Although chiefly nocturnal, the fox will often hunt during the day if it is hungry enough. Its food consists of any bird or mammal it is big enough and quick enough to catch, as well as beetles, snails and some vegetable matter.

Woodcock (*Scolopax rusticola*) WADER FAMILY

Size: Overall length about 13 in. (33 cm). The long bill accounts for about 3 in. (7.6 cm).

Breeding: The hen bird lays from three to four eggs from mid-March onwards. The eggs vary from greyish white, finely speckled with reddish-brown to brown blotched with reddish-brown. The nest is merely a slight hollow in the ground, lined with dead leaves and moss.

The female alone sits on the eggs, which take about 20–21 days to hatch. The welfare and training of the chicks is also her responsibility. The chicks bear quite a strong resemblance to their parents as soon as they are hatched even though they are only covered in downy fluff with the most simplified of markings. They will be able to fly when they are about three weeks old. There are usually two broods a year.

Habits: The most striking feature of this large wader is the eyes. They are black, abnormally large and positioned high and well back in the head, giving all-round vision, thus allowing the woodcock to remain motionless, yet able to keep a watchful eye on its surroundings.

The colour and markings of the male and female are the same and create a wonderful camouflage resembling a pile of dead leaves when the birds are resting in the undergrowth or sitting on the nest.

When disturbed, the woodcock resorts to flight only at the very last moment with a startling sound of vibrating wing beats and flies off at great speed, keeping low and darting left and right through the trees and bushes with an ability equalled by few other birds.

The male woodcock has a most intriguing ritual of flying round and round its territory at sunset and sunrise, just above the tree-tops with slow owl-like wing beats. This performance, known as 'roding', occurs mainly between March and July and probably has something to do with letting other males know that this patch of woodland is his, and to keep off!

Other than during the breeding season, the

woodcock is a very solitary bird. Resting in the cover of the undergrowth by day, it sets forth in the evening to feed in the damp, swampy parts of the woodland. Here it seeks its favourite food, the worm, by plunging its long bill deep down into the soil and catching the worm unawares. As both the upper and lower tips of the bill are flexible, they can be bent outwards and the woodcock is able to swallow the worm without removing its bill from the ground. Other foods sought by the woodcock are insects, grubs and snails which it finds by probing crevices among tree roots and under fallen leaves. Occasionally grass and seeds are eaten.

Woodcock chick

Badger (*Meles meles*) WEASEL FAMILY

Size: Up to 36 in. (91 cm). in length and standing about 12 in. (30 cm) at the shoulder. Weight up to 40 lb (18 kg).

Breeding: The male is known as a boar and the female a sow. They are thought to pair for life. They produce only one family a year. One to five cubs are born during February or March, deep down in the burrow or 'set'. Here they will remain for the first six to eight weeks of their lives before venturing outside the set during the late evenings for their first experience of woodland life.

Like all young mammals, they spend their early life in carefree rough-and-tumble games but after a week or so, they begin to accompany the sow further and further from the set and to learn how to fend for themselves. About October, they leave their parents and set up home for themselves.

Habits: The big, bear-like badger is strictly nocturnal, very secretive and therefore seldom seen by other than the lucky observer. Late one autumn evening, I chanced to spot a boldly marked black and white striped head which popped up from the stinging nettles in the field next to my house – unmistakably a badger.

I decided to sit out the following evening in the hope of seeing it again. So, taking up my position on a groundsheet, I sat and waited . . . for hours. Thoroughly disheartened and stiff with the cold, I decided that home and a nice warming drink would be my only reward for this night's badger watching. On rising to my feet, I chanced to look behind me – and there, some few yards away and watching me intently, sat the badger! By this time, however, the badger had obviously seen enough of me and galloped off into the night.

Amongst themselves, badgers are very sociable and often make family visits to neighbouring sets. Sometimes they stay several days before returning to their own set.

Whenever possible, the set is dug in sandy soil and is a system of large tunnels connecting living chambers and sleeping quarters. A set will have

several entrances and exits from which well worn trails can easily be seen.

The set is always kept beautifully clean. Old bedding is frequently changed for fresh grass, leaves, moss and ferns.

The badger feeds on a wide variety of foods but shows a preference for young rabbits, mice, slugs, beetles, wasps, bees, grubs, berries, roots and acorns.

Green Woodpecker (*Picus viridis*) WOODPECKER FAMILY

Size: Length about 12½ in. (31 cm).

Breeding: The nest is a hole in an old tree trunk. The hole is bored by using its powerful bill and any chips falling into the hole will form the only nesting material. The entrance is made just large enough for the parent birds to squeeze through. Usually five or six white eggs will be laid from about the end of April onwards.

Although aspen and oak seem to be the favourite trees of residence, it will sometimes show a preference for beech, elm and even fir, among others.

The nest may be sited at any height, sometimes only three or four feet (about one metre) from the ground though more usually a much higher position is favoured.

Both parents share the incubation or hatching period as well as the feeding of the family. The eggs hatch in about 15–17 days and the young birds fly when about 18–21 days old.

Only one family is reared each year.

Habits: The green woodpecker is the most colourful of our woodland birds. When seen in its undulating flight with the sunlight glinting through the trees catching its green, yellow and red plumage, the effect is dazzling. A sight perhaps more in keeping with a tropical jungle background than a British woodland. The male and female are alike except the male's mouth stripe is red and the female's is black.

The presence of the green woodpecker is usually heralded by the familiar sound of hammering as it bores into the tree bark. This sound and the sound of its crazy laughing call can be heard all over the woodland. The calls of the green woodpecker are many and varied; some are surprisingly musical and often mistaken for that of the song thrush.

This sturdily built woodpecker is well suited to its life up among the woodland branches. The feet have two toes facing frontwards and two backwards thus enabling it to move with ease and safety over, around and underneath branches. It moves with jerky hops, upwards, sideways and even backwards – but unlike its neighbour the nuthatch, it never goes down head first.

The strongly shafted, rather stiff, tail feathers are kept pressed against the tree for support whilst it probes the bark for the many different kinds of insects found there.

The green woodpecker's food consists of insects, grubs, various seeds, fruits and some vegetable matter. Its favourite dish appears to be the ant. Perhaps this explains why a bird so well suited to life as a tree dweller should spend so much time on the ground, often some distance from the nearest trees.

When feeding on ants it first disturbs them by touching the anthill with its beak and when they begin to rush frantically about in all directions, it simply hangs out its long sticky tongue and allows the ants to stick to it. The tongue is about four times the length of its bill.

When seeking larvae of wood-boring insects deep in the wood, it first chisels down to them with its powerful bill and then uses its long sticky tongue to 'winkle' them out.

Wood Mouse
(*Sylvaemus sylvaticus*)
RODENT FAMILY

Size: Head and body $3\frac{1}{2}$ in. (9 cm). Overall length about 7 in. (18 cm). Weight about $\frac{3}{5}$ oz (17 g).

Breeding: The nest of the wood mouse is a ball-like structure of shredded grass and moss. It is usually in a chamber just off the main underground tunnel. Occasionally the family home will be made under loosely piled stones or twigs or among the roots of a tree. Sometimes an old bird's nest in a hedgerow or high up in a tree will be used. The wood mouse is an excellent climber.

The wood mouse will have five or more litters a year between March and October. Sometimes it breeds right through the winter months if the weather is mild enough.

There are usually about six babies in each litter. They will remain in the nest until about the sixteenth day. By the time they are

21 days old they will have learnt to fend for themselves. They will not, however, move far from their parents as wood mice prefer to live in colonies made up of family units.

Habits: The wood mouse is most active at night. Like many creatures that live a nocturnal life, it has very large dark eyes that enable it to see quite well in the dark.

In daylight however, the wood mouse is very short-sighted. When occasionally it explores for food during the day, it relies almost entirely on its very sensitive hearing and keen sense of smell to find its food and keep out of trouble.

The wood mouse makes many hidden runways under fallen branches, dead leaves and general undergrowth to enable it to move about its business unobserved.

The wood mouse always keeps itself well groomed. It is seen here cleaning its tail.

This very active and agile little mouse appears to be equally at home climbing among the hedgerows as it is on the ground. When climbing trees, however, it is much more cautious and makes its way very carefully from twig to twig. But once on a stouter branch, it will run along with short rapid steps with its tail held high to keep its balance.

When alarmed or in a hurry the wood mouse leaps along in a series of kangaroo-like bounds of up to four feet long (over one metre), sometimes moving so quickly as to be almost impossible to follow with the naked eye. Alas, this incredible turn of speed does not always save the wood mouse because having reached cover it fondly believes, like many of its mouse and vole cousins, that if the head is hidden from view, it cannot be seen. Unhappily, this belief sometimes leaves the rest of the body still very much in view and leads to the downfall of many a mouse!

In snow, the tiny footprints so widely spaced have given rise to many weird and wonderful tales of strange beasts that pass in the night, and are known by many as 'the Devil's footprints'.

The wood mouse feeds on all kinds of seeds, berries, grasses, fungi, flowers, nuts and insects, and even snails are sometimes eaten. As any of this food becomes seasonally plentiful, it is stored away in a 'larder' which is often just an extension to its nest. This 'larder' often contains large quantities of food and is probably used by several members of the same mouse colony.

Nuts eaten by the wood mouse have a hole gnawed in the blunt end.

Tawny Owl (*Strix aluco*) OWL FAMILY

Size: Length about 15 in. (38 cm). The largest owl regularly breeding in the British Isles (see illustration on title-page).

Breeding: There is usually only one brood a year. From two to four, or sometimes as many as seven, white roundish eggs will be laid in March or April.

The nest is a hole in a tree or the disused nest of a crow, magpie or squirrel. No nesting material is used.

When the chicks or 'owlets' are hatched, they are covered in soft downy feathers. The male feeds the female and her babies for the first four to five weeks. The owlets leave the nest at this time but remain with the parents and continue to be fed by them until they are about four months old.

The owlet's natural hunting instincts, however, are displayed at a very early age by their obvious delight in stalking beetles and flies that find their way into the nest, though seldom with any success.

The parent birds are very protective and have been known to attack any person or creature venturing too close to the nest. Egg stealers such as stoats, weasels and members of the crow family are very careful to keep well away from an owl's nest.

Habits: Although no creature can see in total darkness, night creatures like the tawny owl, also known as the brown or wood owl, need less light to see by than those which feed in daylight. Another aid to its nightly activities is its extremely sensitive hearing which can detect a mouse stepping on a dead leaf fifty feet away. Add to these assets the gift of silent flight, due to its plumage and leading edges of the wing feathers being so wonderfully soft, and it is easy to understand why the tawny owl is the most feared of the night hunters.

The brown plumage, richly streaked and mottled with dark brown and black, allows it to blend perfectly with the woodland night. Even when disturbed in daylight, it appears as no more than a silent shadow floating on huge slow beating wings only to disappear completely on reaching the shadows.

Another interesting feature of the owl is the ability to turn its head right round to look

squarely over its back to search the surroundings carefully for a possible meal without moving its body and giving its presence away. Most of its hunting is done by waiting patiently, perched on a branch, for a suitable meal to come along.

The tawny owl has two toes facing forward and two pointing backwards, thus giving it a fearfully powerful grip, strong enough for it to snatch up a young rabbit.

Other foods taken by the tawny owl are small birds, insects, snails, frogs and occasionally fish.

During the day, it roosts in a hollow tree or perches on a branch close to the trunk, preferably covered with ivy to hide from noisy little birds that mob it and disturb its slumbers.

At dusk it sets out on its night's work calling 'kewick' often repeated several times. The most familiar call however, is the spooky spine-chilling 'Hoo-hoo-hoooooo' which echoes across all the woodland and is fair warning to all those about, to be ever watchful.

Red Squirrel
(*Sciurus vulgaris*) RODENT FAMILY

Size: Overall length about $15\frac{1}{2}$ in. (39 cm). Weight 8–10 oz (220–280 g).

Breeding: The red squirrel usually has about three or four babies in a litter. They are born between January and April. A further family may be born between May and August. The young remain with their parents until fully grown.

Baby squirrels are born in a nest or 'drey' high up in a tree. Oc-casionally they may be born in a hollow tree. The drey is a very bulky loose con-struction of twigs, bark, leaves and moss. Sometimes the drey is built around the old

Nursery nest

nest of a crow or magpie. Some are domed, others cup-shaped. The squirrel will build several dreys, all within a few trees of one another. One will serve as a nursery while the others will be used as resting places. The breeding nest is larger and more ball-like.

Habits: The red squirrel, like its cousin, the grey squirrel, is the supreme 'high wire' perfor-mer of the woodland. Full of fun, it runs swiftly along the top, the side, underneath, up, down and around branches and tree trunks with breathtaking agility.

This acrobatic ability is made possible because the long hind-legs and shorter fore-legs are superbly muscled and give the squirrel abnormal strength for its size.

In marked contrast to its frequent bursts of energy, the squirrel can sit motionless for long periods, to blend perfectly with its background.

The loud call of 'chuck, chuck, chuck' will often give the unseen squirrel's presence away.

Although the squirrel is a shy creature, it can be enticed to take food from the hand. One cheeky young squirrel became so bold after a while that he would regularly tap on my window until I fed him with his favourite breakfast of peanuts.

In winter the red squirrel grows its rather splendid ear tufts and becomes slightly less active, though it doesn't hibernate. At most it tends to take extended naps, frequently waking on fine days to feed and catch up on woodland life.

The red squirrel's food consists of nuts, cones, berries, fruit and fungi, much of which is gathered and stored for the coming winter months. These food stores, dug just below the surface of the ground, rarely contain more than one nut or berry as

Grey squirrel

The squirrel gnaws a hole in the top of the shell to reach the nut inside.

the squirrel seems to prefer several small 'larders' rather than the one big one favoured by the wood mouse. Unfortunately having so many larders, it tends to forget where most of them are. The squirrel will also raid nests to take eggs and young birds.

The strong incisor teeth with which the squirrel gnaws through nut shells, grow continuously. They are kept at their useful length by grinding the upper and lower teeth together, a pastime which appears to give the squirrel much pleasure.

In recent years, the red squirrel has declined in numbers and is now found only in a few areas of Wales, the West Country, East Anglia, some Northern counties, Scotland and Ireland.

Wood Pigeon (*Columba palumbus*) PIGEON FAMILY

Size: Length about 16 in. (40 cm). Wing span about 18 in. (46 cm). This is the largest pigeon found in this country.

Breeding: The courtship or billing and cooing of the parent birds consists of a head-on approach of strutting, bowing the head and puffing out the breast feathers. At times, they become so excited that one or both birds may be pushed off the branch.

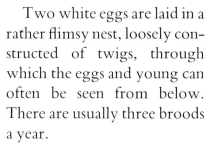

Two white eggs are laid in a rather flimsy nest, loosely constructed of twigs, through which the eggs and young can often be seen from below. There are usually three broods a year.

The male collects the nest materials while the female spends her time actually building the nest. Both birds share the responsibility of incubation and feeding. The parent birds produce a fluid known as 'Pigeon's Milk' from their crops. The chick receives this by plunging its head into the parent's mouth and the milk is 'pumped' in. The young remain in the nest for about three weeks and continue to be fed by the parents until they are about four weeks old.

The chick is the ugliest little creature imaginable and in no way resembles the handsome bird it will grow into.

Habits: The wood pigeon is one of the most numerous of woodland birds. During the summer months they go around on their own or in pairs, occasionally in small groups. At other times however, they gather into large flocks, sometimes numbering many hundreds.

The wood pigeon has been furnished with a very large crop in which to store food before it passes on to be digested. This crop needs constantly 'stocking up', so the pigeon is always busily foraging for all kinds of seeds, green stuff, berries, nuts and even insects both on the ground and in the trees.

The wood pigeon is one of the woodland's early warning systems. At the first hint of anything unusual, it will take to flight with a startling frantic rustling of leaves and branches accompanied by a loud clapping of wings. This will alert every creature within earshot and any hope of slipping into the wood unobserved is quickly shattered. Nevertheless, all is forgiven as there is

nothing quite so pleasant as the sound of it softly cooing on a warm summer's afternoon.

Common Dormouse (*Muscardinus avellanarius*) RODENT FAMILY

Size: Overall length $5\frac{1}{2}$–$6\frac{1}{2}$ in. (14–17 cm). The bushy tail accounts for about half this length. Weight $\frac{3}{5}$ oz–$1\frac{1}{2}$ oz (17–42 g). The enormous difference in weight for such a tiny creature is due to excessive eating to put on weight to help sustain it during its hibernation from October to April. During this time about half its body weight will be lost.

Breeding: The dormouse has several litters each year of between three and seven young ones.

The first litter arrives in spring or early summer. Occasionally a litter may be born as late as October. Unfortunately, these late offspring stand little chance of putting on enough body weight to sustain them through the long winter hibernation, and so seldom survive.

The nursery nest is ball-like, about 6 in. (15 cm) in diameter and made of loosely woven grass, moss, leaves, bark and twigs or any combination of these materials and may be situated among tree roots, hedgerows, in a hollow tree or high up in the bushes.

At six weeks old, the young dormouse will be fully grown and quite independent.

Habits: The common dormouse looks rather like a cross between a mouse and a squirrel. Very agile, it confidently climbs about among the trees and bushes, and even makes occasional squirrel-like leaps from one twig to another.

Being naturally rather plump, it finds all this activity rather exhausting and frequently returns to the nest for a little nap. It is undoubtedly the sleepiest little creature in all the woodland and is often known as 'sleepmouse', 'sleepy mouse', 'dozy mouse' and other sleepy names.

Though its huge dark eyes are those of a strictly nocturnal animal it is probably more active at dawn and dusk. The periods of 'dozing off' between bouts of activity get longer and longer as winter draws near until, by about October, the dormouse doesn't wake up at all and will sleep right round to next April!

During this hibernation, the dormouse will occasionally wake up just long enough to take a little food before dozing off again. It is the only British rodent to hibernate.

The nest into which it retires during the day is about half the size of the nursery nest but of similar construction. During hibernation however, it forsakes both these nests for one situated under a pile of leaves or stones, among tree roots, or sometimes underground in a disused burrow.

The dormouse is a most enchanting little

creature and will behave in much the same way as a squirrel even to sitting up on its haunches to nibble a nut held delicately in its fore paws. When fast asleep it still presents an appealing picture – rolled up with chin on tummy, fore paws folded over its nose with the bushy tail wrapped around the head . . . a tiny, fat, furry ball.

The dormouse feeds largely on nuts with a marked preference for hazel nuts. It also eats seeds, berries, fruit, young shoots, bark, as well as insects, snails and the occasional egg or baby bird if given the opportunity.

As winter draws near, the dormouse gathers in extra food to put by in case it wakes up feeling hungry during hibernation. Some of this food may well have been stolen, for the dormouse is not above sneaking into another animal's food store, if the owner isn't about, and adding some of it to its own larder!

Ken Lilly
'76

Nuthatch (*Sitta europaea*) NUTHATCH FAMILY

Size: 5½ in. (14 cm).

Breeding: Four to six eggs, sometimes as many as twelve, will be laid in April or May. The eggs are white, strongly spotted with reddish brown. There is usually only one family or 'brood' each year.

A hole in a tree is used for the nest, or perhaps a disused magpie's nest. The nest may be found at any height, sometimes only a few feet (about a metre) from the ground. The nuthatch doesn't seem to care very much about where the nest is – providing it makes a good family home. If it finds the entrance too big, it will use mud to plaster round the edge to reduce the size to its liking.

The nest may be lined with flaked bark, dead grass and leaves. Sometimes no nesting material is used at all.

The young are fed mainly on insects by both parents and will remain in the nest for about 25 days.

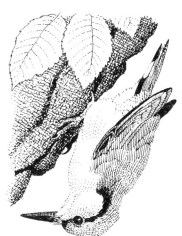

Habits: The nuthatch is a noisy, plump, woodpecker-like little bird, constantly repeating its call of 'chwit chwit' with some variations and is known as the woodlands' little chatterbox.

Always active, it moves with jerky hops upwards, sideways, downwards, head first or tail first, busily probing the bark crevices for insects. It rarely feeds on the ground.

The nuthatch feeds on nuts and is particularly fond of hazel nuts. It also eats a wide variety of seeds and insects. When feeding on nuts, it wedges the nut firmly in the fork of a branch or deep crevice in the bark. Then, gripping the bark firmly with its strong claws, it leans far back before swinging down with the whole weight of its body. It strikes the shell with its powerful bill time and time again until the shell breaks and the nut inside can be reached.

The slow, often erratic rhythm of these hammer-like blows can be heard for some distance and is quite different from the more rapid machine-gun-like tapping of the woodpecker.

Stoat (*Mustela erminea*)

WEASEL FAMILY

Size: Length about 14–17 in. (35–43 cm) including 4½ in. (11 cm) of tail. The males tend to be a little larger than the females. Weight 5–16 oz (140–450 g).

Breeding: The stoat makes its home in a hole in a bank, or under tree roots, or in the hollow of a tree. The baby stoats are born in April or May. There may be as few as four or as many as nine in a litter, of which there is only one a year. They are weaned when about five weeks old. Throughout this time, the mother cares for and feeds the family.

The stoat, always courageous in defence of its rights, will defend its young to the death.

The young often stay with their parents and hunt in family groups. Sometimes two or more families will join forces to form large 'packs'. There are stories told by countrymen of these 'packs' attacking dogs and even men!

Habits: The stoat is one of the most feared of all the hunters. Won-

derfully agile and active, it spends almost every waking moment seeking its prey down in holes and burrows, along river banks and, being an excellent swimmer, often taking to the water in its travels, and climbing trees with the nimbleness of a squirrel. It moves about in undergrowth and open ground in a series of long, low bounds in a rather snake-like manner, frequently stopping for a moment or two to raise its head to catch the scent or sound of anything interesting before eagerly moving on.

The stoat hunts mainly at night. When it occasionally hunts by day, because its eyesight is rather poor, it relies almost entirely upon its amazingly keen sense of smell and hearing to locate its prey.

Its food consists of any creature it can over-power. Many of its victims fear the stoat so much that even the scent of it on the breeze can reduce the unfortunate creature to a state of paralysed fear, so that it does not even attempt to defend itself or run away. Once the stoat has moved in to within a few feet (about a metre) of its prey, the final dash into the 'kill' is made with such breathtaking speed as to be almost impossible for the eye to follow.

Nevertheless, the stoat does not always meet with success in its ventures and occasionally the tables are turned. Some years ago, my grand-father, returning home one evening, saw a rabbit cross the lane ahead of him, closely pursued by a stoat. They both disappeared down into the ditch and, on hearing an agonising scream, my grand-father hurried forward and prodded about in the weed-covered ditch with his stick confidently expecting to take a freshly killed rabbit home to grandma but no . . . what he found was the stoat lying with its neck broken and quite dead.

During the winter in more northerly colder districts, the stoat changes its rich reddy-brown summer coat for a beautiful white wintery one. When this happens, the stoat is known as the 'ermine'. However, whichever coat it may wear, it always shows a black tip to its tail.

Index

To find out more about the birds and mammals in this book and where to go and watch them, the local public library can usually not only recommend books on each subject but can supply addresses of the local wildlife and conservation societies. These societies are always willing to offer help and guidance to anyone wishing to know more about the subject. The libraries should also be able to help as to where there are woods in the area owned by the Forestry Commission, the Nature Conservancy and the National Trust, which are open to the public.

Remember before you enter a wood, always make certain that it is open to the public or, if the woodland is privately owned, you have the owner's permission to be there. Do not strike a light or light fires. (Serious fires have been started by cigarette ends.) Remember the ever present fire hazard in woodland and of course be careful to leave gates as you find them. Then, once in the wood, the golden rule, if you hope to see the animals going about their daily business, is to be quiet, ever watchful and very, very patient.